How to Marry
A Fabulous
Man

by Pari Livermore

∕∕∕eredith ®
■■■ ▌ B O O K S
Meredith Books
1716 Locust Street
Des Moines, Iowa 50309–3023
meredithbooks.com

First Edition.
Printed in China
Library of Congress Control Number: 2007921723
ISBN: 978-0-696-23675-4

Just ♥ ♥
♥ ♥ Married

contents

Acknowledgments

I read once that one out of every five Americans is reading a book and the other four are writing one. Few finish writing a book, and those who do have so many people to thank. In my case, I would especially like to express my appreciation to Ron Gordon for challenging me to complete *How to Marry a Fabulous Man*; he was incredibly supportive along the way.

Going much farther back, I am indebted to my grandmother, Emma Davis, who helped spark a little girl's interest in literature, and my father, Ted Caldwell, who taught me the joy of writing. My friends who believed in me and helped me more than I can say are Catherine Debs, Janet Fox, Linda Breitstone, and Linda Hothem. When my friend Gail Glasser, who has incredibly great taste, told me how much she loved the book, it gave me encouragement. I felt confident enough to ask my pal Barbara Carey to introduce me to her literary agent, Bill Gladstone. Barbara and I both believe he walks on water. His special kind of matching paired me with the warm and encouraging people at Meredith Books. Lisa Berkowitz is my champion and she helped my dreams become reality. Vicki Christian was an insightful project manager with amazing sensitivity.

Many thanks to Mia Wyant, Marsha Hallerud, and Irina Cordell who helped me with the typing and proofreading and let me bounce ideas

ideas off them. I owe a mega thank you to Patrick Siu from CIPA Graphics who has a very romantic soul and who helped set the artistic direction for this book. Leslie Harlib and Rhonda Carpenter deserve a big hand for helping me with the grammar and editing. And it has been my great honor to work with my publicist Sandi Mendelson from Hilsinger Mendelson East. She really knows how to get the job done!

I would also like to thank the most important people in my life. My mother, Phyllis Caldwell, whose kindness I always strive to emulate, and my husband, Putnam Livermore. When I was a small child, I used to dream about what my husband would be like, what he would say and do. But even my wildest imaginings could not conjure up the wonderful man I married.

I owe a debt of gratitude to the thousands of women I have worked with over the years. I have introduced them to lots of men and gained so much wisdom from watching them find happiness. They helped me learn the very best ways to marry a fabulous man.

Television documentaries, magazines, and radio interviews have proclaimed me one of the nation's top matchmakers. Some of the most high-powered couples in the country have turned to me for help. Every day I speak to men about what they want in a woman and they tell me the same things over and over again.

I've been there when women have made mistakes and I've been there when they've done all the right things. I'd like to share these winning secrets with you. If you can master two or three of the tips every week, you'll meet a lot more men and develop much better dating skills.

Finding the right person requires as much effort as looking for a job. If you put in the time and adopt these habits, there is no question you can marry a fabulous man. Don't forget to invite me to the wedding!

—Pari Livermore

ready:
How to Meet The
Best Men

If the man you just met reminds you of Brad Pitt, but he doesn't have the qualities you want—throw that fish back!

"*If you can't name it, you can't claim it.*"

—Brianna Morley, pastry chef and one of Pari's successful matches

If you can't articulate your goals, you can't achieve them. It's much easier to get married if you know what kind of man you want. Have you ever made a list of the qualities you would truly admire in a partner? Try it. Then circle the three most important. Once you feel sure enough of your list, concentrate on dating only men who have these qualities and avoiding men who don't. Try not to focus on the wrong issues.

If he has what you want, but he looks like Elmer Fudd, don't pass him by. When Sylvia, a former New York newscaster, met Bob, she said he reminded her of a chubby cartoon character. In a few weeks he captured her heart and became her hero. I've seen it happen many times. As you begin to care about someone, his appearance becomes less important.

On the other hand if the man you just met reminds you of Brad Pitt but he doesn't have the other qualities you want—throw that fish back! There will be plenty of other women who will want him. He will only make you unhappy and your unhappiness will make him miserable. No man likes to feel that he is not enough. (Or no woman either, for that matter.)

*"You never get a
second chance to make
a first impression."* —Eleanor Roosevelt

It is important to remember that men are very visual. Try to look as GOOD as possible as OFTEN as possible. You never know when you'll meet someone just perfect for you, even if you're just stopping at the library, cleaners, or gas station. When it happens, you don't want to be worrying about the spot on your blouse, your raggedy shoes, or your two inches of black roots. If you know you look terrific, you'll feel confident.

One young teacher I know realized that the only eligible men who came her way were the men she jogged with every morning. She bought a hot jogging outfit and got up 10 minutes early to put on lipstick and comb her hair.

Three weeks later she met her husband, a guy she had passed on the track every morning. She said, "He never noticed me before." He said, "She never noticed me." They agreed that the few minutes she spent getting ready for her jog gave her the confidence to smile at him, and he took it from there.

Wear Something Terrific on First Dates

Just to be safe choose black. It goes anywhere, makes you look slimmer, and you can dress it up or down. You can wear it with everything, and it's easy to accessorize. If you don't look good in black, try camel, gray, or bone.

Your outfit should fit like a glove. Use great care in choosing the dress or trousers. Don't skimp on the cost. It should be as expensive as your salary will allow and not an impulse purchase. You should feel beautiful each time you put it on. Make sure whatever you wear is in excellent shape. Dry-clean it if you need to and see that hems are even and buttons secure.

A timeless style will appeal to the most men. Stay away from too trendy, too sexy, or too showy. Shoes and accessories should be perfect and in good repair. Men are very visual, so your outfit should tastefully highlight your best physical assets. When you get up from the table, his admiration for your figure and style should remain with him long afterward.

Visualize Your Success

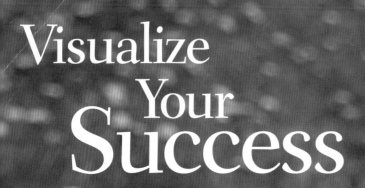

Celia, a blond bombshell who worked for the mayor's office, decided it was the right time to get married. She chose the date and nightly visualized the type of man she wanted to marry. Celia was clear that her husband would be a man of great honesty and integrity. She knew she was ready and was sure everything would fall into place.

Celia visualized where she would live and walked her dog in that neighborhood. She even surprised the astounded mayor when she asked him to officiate at her wedding to an as yet unknown beau. When she met her husband, Jacob, Celia was convinced he was the right one before the end of their first date. "I was positive before I drove out of the driveway!" she exclaimed. "When you are sure about what you want, you'll find it almost instantly!" When Celia and Jacob married, the mayor officiated. Could it happen to you?

Visualization really works. Once I attended a service at the Marble Collegiate Church in New York City, where the Rev. Norman Vincent Peale, author of the book *The Power of Positive Thinking*, told the congregation a story.

"There were three basketball teams," he said, "all playing at the same level. They decided to experiment. For one month Team A practiced four days a week. Team B did not practice. And Team C? They sat in front of the basket and visualized themselves scoring every time. After a month Team C put in the best performance."

There is scientific proof that visualization works. It's even used as a treatment for cancer. The idea is if you can picture yourself doing something, it's more likely to happen. If you think positively and see all the details of a successful courtship and beautiful wedding, you can conjure up a fabulous husband.

Write Your Own Commercial

Include 10 areas in which you excel. This is a terrific exercise to help you understand just how great you are. Make an audiotape and play it back before you start each day. Make a copy of it for your car and play it during traffic jams. Make a toast to yourself each week and repeat your commercial. Here's what I did for myself: "I'm an excellent matchmaker and I really enjoy bringing happiness to other people. I give fabulous parties and I try to be warm and friendly.

"People tell me I have good written and verbal communication skills and I enjoy interacting with people. I am creative and artistic. I am a practical idealist.

"My friends say I'm a great cook and I experiment with very unusual recipes. When I entertain, my guests seem to be delighted with my beautiful table displays."

This may sound egotistic, but if you write down all your best qualities and repeat them over and over, you will learn to believe in yourself!

Don't put everyone else first and yourself second. Here are some beautiful words from the Jewish Talmud: "If I am not for myself, then who is for me?" Realize what an outstanding woman you are. Learn to appreciate your amazing abilities and accomplishments.

"*Put on a happy face.*"

—*from the musical* Bye Bye Birdie

Men always insist they want a happy woman. Everybody has baggage. Until you really get to know each other, leave yours at home. When I was 18 my sister's best friend, Nancy, gave me some terrific advice. "When you start dating someone, don't divulge all your problems," she confided. "He should think everything is perfect. After a few months you can say, 'Well, I'm really happy, but I do have this little problem.' If he doesn't go away, then after a few more months you can say, 'Well, there is this other little problem,' and you just keep on disclosing information every few months until you've told him everything he needs to know."

Some women make the mistake of thinking, "I really like this guy so I'm going to be totally honest with him. I'm going to tell him all my deep dark secrets right away."

They spend their first date talking about all their deep darks and by the end of the evening he knows the bad things and almost none of the good. Smarter women will spend their first dates highlighting some of their finer qualities and never mention any personal problems.

Give a Party

I f you're acquainted with a man who has some terrific friends or if you've noticed the fellow next door has some great buddies, suggest a get-together. You invite the women; he invites the men. Describe your friends in the best possible light so he'll be enthusiastic about the party. Be specific about what type of men you'd like him to invite. When my female accountant did this, she requested guys with a sense of humor. When her business partner gave such a party, she wanted athletic, Ivy League types.

Share the expenses. Ask the men to bring the liquor and ask the ladies to bring the food. Blow up colorful balloons and write invitations on the surfaces with a ballpoint pen.

When the balloons are deflated, the letters will be shiny and look as if they have been engraved. Voila! You'll have a party for the price of some stamps, envelopes, and balloons.

"Just because you get on the bus doesn't mean you have to go to the end of the line."

—Jana Miller, former airline executive and
one of Pari's successful matches

Don't be shy about dating a man you're unsure of. If there is something you like about him, give it a try. Just because you have a few dates doesn't mean you're on the express bus to the altar.

When you're in a casual dating relationship, you owe each other nothing. We all take our chances. Sometimes you eat the bear and sometimes the bear eats you. Don't keep score. Just have a good time.

You might learn something interesting such as the best sushi joint in town, the best store to buy good, inexpensive wine, or even how to fly-fish. Create some beautiful memories and you'll melt the heart of almost any man.

Dinner for Eight

Have dinner for eight. Combine talents with one of your single friends and have a fabulous dinner party. You should both invite single people the other doesn't know. No couples allowed. Include four exciting women and four exciting men and choose a fun, reasonably priced restaurant. Find one with great food and great acoustics so everyone can talk. Try changing places for the second course. Go Dutch treat. I'll bet it won't be the only time you will want to do this.

"I've been on so many blind dates, I should get a free dog."

—Wendy Liebman, comedian

Make a list of 10 of your most interesting friends. Call them and ask them to introduce you to someone special. Never say, "I haven't had a date in two years." Or, "Guys just don't seem to notice me." Let them know that men sincerely like you and you really enjoy them as well. No one wants to introduce their friends to someone who isn't popular with men.

Recycle

It's hard not to feel a little jealous, but try trading your old boyfriends. If your friend dated a guy briefly but nothing worked out, ask her to introduce him to you. Remember, this will only work if she's over him and if you reciprocate by introducing her to one of your old flames. This takes a generous heart, but it's worth the bit of jealousy that might sting you temporarily. Try keeping your eye on the big picture. This method has tons of benefits; if he falls for her, you can always ask them to find someone for you.

Don't Worry

"Bill will never get married." "Chuck is too old to start a family." "Mark is a real heartbreaker." Don't listen to gossip about the man you're dating. Lauren Bacall once said, "Men are like fish. They all get caught in the end. It just depends on what bait you use."

If you think a man really cares for you, give him the benefit of the doubt. For instance, if a man has been a bachelor for a long time, he may have met a lot of women who have a lot to say about him. He may be everybody's "guy that got away."

When I was dating my husband, we were invited to the home of a prominent socialite who had seen my husband with a different woman every year. As she took my coat, she cautioned, "I hope you don't think this man is going to marry you. You aren't the only goodlooking woman he's ever dated." It stopped me in my tracks, but I whispered, "Yes! But he's never met anyone like me." I now delight in going to her frequent parties. I'm always as sweet as I can possibly be. Many people will try to burst your bubble when you're dating a spectacular man. If you don't act like you're the flavor of the month, you won't be perceived as one.

Exercise And Keep Fit

Thankfully not all men like the same body types. No matter what size and shape you are, there will be guys out there who think you have an amazing figure. Your job is to find one of them. Keep in mind, however, that most men like women who care enough about themselves to exercise and stay in shape, no matter what their body type. Your exercise program doesn't have to include an expensive gym—even just walking 30 minutes three or four times a week is great. You could also jog or try a stationary bike (a punster girlfriend of mine refers to that as "the ride to nowhere"). If you bring your iPod it will make the time go faster. Be sure to get your doctor's consent before you start any exercise program. And get an exercise partner if you can—it makes the task so much more fun.

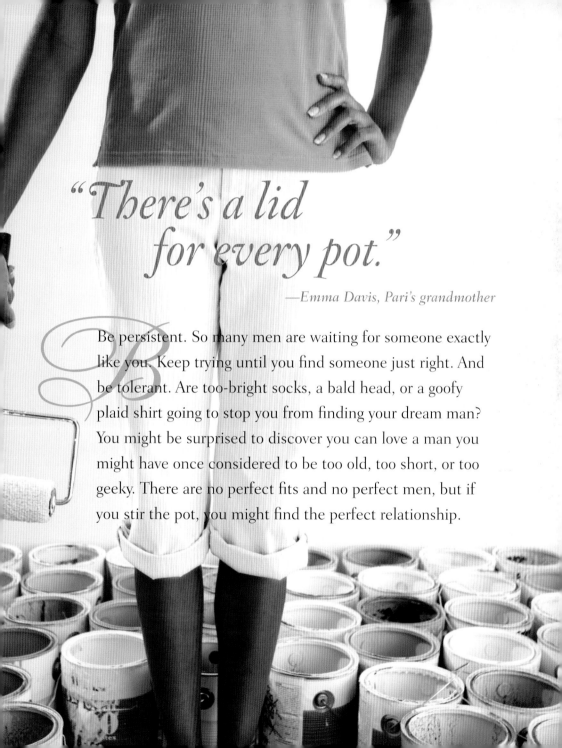

"There's a lid for every pot."

—*Emma Davis, Pari's grandmother*

Be persistent. So many men are waiting for someone exactly like you. Keep trying until you find someone just right. And be tolerant. Are too-bright socks, a bald head, or a goofy plaid shirt going to stop you from finding your dream man? You might be surprised to discover you can love a man you might have once considered to be too old, too short, or too geeky. There are no perfect fits and no perfect men, but if you stir the pot, you might find the perfect relationship.

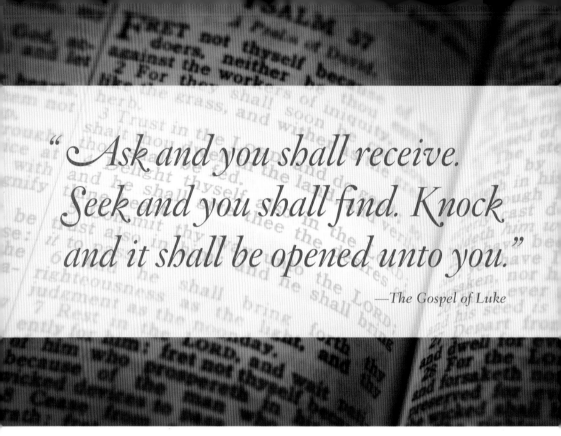

"*Ask and you shall receive. Seek and you shall find. Knock and it shall be opened unto you.*"

—*The Gospel of Luke*

Pray about it. If you're a person of faith, you may want to spend some extra time in your church, mosque, or synagogue. Find out if your house of worship has a singles group. If they don't, volunteer to start one. The Internet has some excellent religious-based matchmaking services you can investigate. If you're Jewish, JDate.com is a particularly good one, or if you're Christian, try ChristianSingles.com. No matter what your religion, there's a site for you if you're looking for a potential lifetime mate.

Just Show Up!

Change your mindset and pick up some new behaviors. Go everywhere, do everything, and join every organization that sounds interesting.

Whenever you meet new people, be nice to everyone. Let them know you're single.

If you walk into a meeting or a party and think there are no possible candidates, be friendly. Reach out to everyone. You can never tell who might have an eligible brother, neighbor, or business partner. Be your charming self and let people know you would appreciate their help.

It's human nature to want to help singles meet one another.

It's human nature to want to help single people meet one another. In days gone by it was considered the responsibility of society to do so. Remind yourself that many married couples were introduced to each other through mutual friends.

Enjoy Dining Alone

Do you come home from work, zap a frozen dinner in the microwave, turn on the TV, and feed the cat? Maybe it's time for a change!

One evening, roommates Ellen and Christine went to a cozy neighborhood French restaurant instead of ordering out. A friendly older woman was having a family birthday party. She offered the pair some chocolate whipped cream birthday cake and introduced Christine to her son and Ellen to her nephew. Each couple began dating and eventually fell in love. Within the year both couples wed. That's how Christine and Ellen went from being best friends to being relatives. They advise, "The love of your life won't come knocking on your door. You'll have to go out and find him."

Your time and effort will bring you success. Marsha, a 40-year-old airline executive, met her husband by dining alone in restaurants. She claims men will approach you more often if you're by yourself. Here are some of her tips:

- **Enter the restaurant with as much confidence as a duchess.** Don't think, "Are people going to wonder why I'm by myself?" Think, "I belong here. They're going to love me."

- **Bring a book to read.** Occasionally look up from it. Appear approachable but don't look as if you're hoping someone will talk to you. Stare a little and try to break the ice with your eyes.

- **Start a conversation** with people sitting near you. You'll meet more people if you sit at the bar or a table for four or six.

- **Check your watch frequently** and pretend you're waiting for someone. This gives men a deadline. They'll think, "I'd better talk to her now before her friends show up."

Start looking today—you'll find Mr. Right. Being a little aggressive can be unattractive when you're dating but it's effective when you're just looking. A reminder: Be friendly and smile a lot.

"Matchmaker, matchmaker, make me a match."

—*from the musical* Fiddler on the Roof

I have one suggestion that will benefit your social life more than any other: Become an amateur matchmaker. If you introduce your friends, there are some big payoffs. Everyone will love you. People can't resist someone who takes a sincere interest in them. You can make some pretty good matches and some wonderful lifelong friendships. Here are some tips so you can become expert at it:

- **Ask questions.** Listen carefully to what someone is looking for. Try to be as fair as possible. You must make someone comfortable enough to be honest with you.

- **Don't be judgmental.** If someone tells you he only likes tall blonds, don't try to convince him to fall in love with a short brunette.

- **Don't become emotionally involved.** If someone doesn't want to date your best friend or there's someone else you think is perfect for him, don't let it bother you.

- **Don't tell secrets.** There is a code among matchmakers (even amateur ones) that you don't share anything intimate. Trust is important.

- **Meet lots of people** so you will have as large a matching pool as possible.

- **Always call in your markers.** You're not getting paid and you're doing a few nice things for a few nice people. So don't be shy about asking them to help you with your social life.

If you fix up enough people, half the city will be out looking for the perfect man for you. You'll be invited to all the great parties, interview for all the best jobs, and you'll almost never sit home on Saturday night.

Get Online

T ry the Internet. One of the better sites is Dr. Phil's "Chemistry" at Match.com. There are many other services that can assist you in finding romance online and there are scads of success stories out there.

eHarmony.com claims it's responsible for matching 33,000 people annually. For people who are looking for someone with common interests, Jim Tracy, publisher of *Online Dating* magazine, suggests investigating niche websites. Some of the most popular sites provide matches for Trekkies, politicos, and animal lovers. These are just a few.

Don't cheat! You may secure some first dates with such tactics, but men won't come back if they catch you fibbing. Be honest about your statistics.

The first few times you meet your cyberdates, don't go alone and don't give out your last name, your cell phone number, or your address. Make sure you meet in public places. Never invite a stranger into your home.

Exercise caution. Do a little sleuthing. Learn all about these men, particularly about their marital status, because there is a downside. Internet sites have lots of problems with married interlopers and even convicted criminals. One flight attendant confided, "I thought I met this awesome guy, but I discovered later that he and the truth were strangers."

I've got...
Steam Heat!

—*from the musical* The Pajama Game

When a man appeals to you, why not flirt, tease, or make a little conversation? You may spot a single guy at the meat counter in your local grocery store. Ask, "Do you know what to look for when you buy a roast?" If he's at the checkout with a six-pack of beer, chips, nuts, and plastic tableware, ask, "Where's the party?"

Other good places to meet eligible men are the library (ask if they've read the latest best seller) or bookstores, where you can sip coffee and browse. Follow your interests and hobbies so if you do meet a man, you'll have something fun in common.

It shouldn't be news to you that a man must be sexually attracted to a woman before he wants to see her again. So it helps if you're sending vibes that let him know you're interested. So flirt. The train won't leave the station until you get that engine started.

Put Down That Phone!

It's OK to be subtly aggressive (just one phone call or one email) when you're trying to get a man's attention. Or tell his friends you think he's gorgeous. Surprisingly this really works.

You can also invite him to join you at a dinner party or social function, preferably not as your date, but as one of the gang. Afterward, don't contact him unless he contacts you. If you must reach him, there should always be a purpose for your call, letter, or email. Until your relationship is exclusive, never call just to chat. Even then do it sparingly. Remember, men need a challenge to conquer. What our mamas said is still true: Don't be too available.

Give Back

Why not meet some wonderful people and help charitable causes at the same time? There are many nonprofit organizations in your community that need your help. If you are feeling blue because you haven't met anyone, the best way to keep from being sad is to help someone else.

Assess what skills you have to help a worthy cause. Join an organization you'd like to support. Rosalie, a hair colorist, decided to help a children's group in Seattle. While she was skating at an ice rink with one of the kids, she bumped into Jim, an electrical engineer who literally swept her off her feet. Denise, the little girl she was teaching to skate, announced, "You two are going to get married." And they did!

So go ahead. Sign up to serve dinner at the homeless shelter. Get involved with your church's mission group. Volunteer to read to the blind or the elderly at your local hospital. Who knows? You might meet your special someone while you're helping others.

"Let them see what you got, but don't let them have it."

—Gypsy Rose Lee, entertainer

Try to recall the compliments men have given you about your figure. Every woman should know what part of her body is most enticing and, by all means, celebrate it with style. Don't wear clothing that is too provocative. Showing too much skin may send the wrong message. Show the form but not the flesh.

"Hey there, you with the
stars in your eyes."

—*from the musical* The Pajama Game

In a crowded room, especially at a party, it's OK to stare. Don't be afraid to give a guy the "go ahead" sign. Most men appreciate an approachable woman. Let him know you like him. Show your interest, but don't chase him. Smile and when he catches your eye, look down, and then look away. Act sweet and a little shy, but get your point across. Being slightly embarrassed at getting caught looking at a man can be very charming.

When you see a stranger across the room give the man permission to approach you with "The 3-Second Smile," says dating coach Dr. Gayle Delaney. "Let him know you want to meet him," she says. "Look at him and repeat three sentences to yourself: 'You're handsome. I'd like to get to know you. Why don't you say hello?'"

My friend Susan went to school with Hillary Rodham Clinton. Susan was always amused by what she observed to be the "Hillary Hello." She often caught the future New York senator flirting across the room with her eyes. Would you like to marry a president?

On the day the Clintons first met at the Yale Law School library, they stared at each other for almost half an hour. Finally Hillary walked across the room to meet Bill. Her opening line was, "We may as well introduce ourselves if we are going to continue to stare at one another." Maybe great eye contact can turn you into a first lady or even a future president.

Hit the Hot Spots

When you attend cocktail parties, have you ever noticed there is always a group of people standing together that look like they are having the most fun? Why not join them? Stand as close to them as possible.

If there are other similar clusters in the room, try blending into those groups too. Start at the outside edge, talking to the people who aren't quite in the absolute center of the action.

Yolanda had just moved to Seattle and was looking for a job. She joined a group of singles at a cocktail party in her building.

She started talking to a chubby fellow on the edge of the group. He was getting the cold shoulder from a sexy-looking blond. Yolanda was so sweet and so charming to that man, before she knew what was happening, everyone wanted to meet her. The new girl in town had landed smack dab in the middle of the hot spot. Within 24 hours she had a job interview and two dates for the following weekend.

When you're thinking hot spots, don't limit yourself to the latest trendy bar or party. Go to a jazz performance at a blues club, a new exhibition at the art center, or a cat or dog show. You'll meet interesting men and learn something new too.

Remember: Smile and be friendly. If you're interesting and interested, you just might become the center of interest yourself.

"*Follow the fellow who follows a dream.*"

—*from the musical* Finian's Rainbow

If you want to be happy, figure out what contribution you can make to this world, then put your ideas into action. It's not good enough just to have the dream. You must have the drive to go along with it or your dreams won't come true. If you're following your dreams, men will find you a lot more interesting.

In the same way, if you find a man with a big dream that has come true or is about to come true, life can become exhilarating. Ask the men you meet about their dreams. The more details they give you about them, the greater chance they have of fulfilling them.

But watch out for the big talkers. If he's out partying until the wee hours, if he works indoors but always has a great tan, or if he spends every spare minute playing golf or tennis, he's probably doing more talking than working. If he's not going to put in the time, he's not going to get the job done.

Unleash
Your Inner Tomboy

Men love athletic women. To appeal to the greatest number of guys, you should have at least one sport in which you excel. If you don't, start simply. Buy a backpack and learn to hike. To keep it honest, hoof it to the dry cleaners, mall, and grocery store. A bonus: You'll get healthier.

Never say, "I'm really not very athletic" or "I'm not interested in sports." Your goal should be to appeal to the most men. If you're not active in one sport, athletic guys will wonder what you've been doing for the last 20, 30, or even 40 years. They may also question what else you don't do.

Good places to meet men are volleyball games, golf and tennis courts, and running events. Linda, a social worker with a knockout figure and legs that won't quit, met her husband, Ron, at a footrace. He's a tall, blond, successful real estate developer. Weeks later Linda beat him in a triathlon by five minutes. Ron fell in love with her mind and her athletic ability. They've been married 11 years, and even after having two kids, he still chases her around the bedroom.

If your budget can support it, join a fitness club, where men still usually outnumber women. Try weight training and ask the closest hunk to spot you. Who knows what could happen?

If you want to appeal to a prince, look at Kate Middleton, former girlfriend of England's Prince William. She's proficient in hockey, tennis, swimming, skiing, and running. These skills enhanced her appeal as a possible mate for the future King of England.

Be Extraordinary

If you just spent $75 on a hot little haircut, stopped at Saks for advice on makeup, and bought a stunning new dress, don't stop there! A man may be crazy about the cover, but he has to love the book. You have to be the book that intrigues him, challenges him, and takes his mind off his troubles.

Think of yourself as an uncut diamond, polishing each facet. The more you offer, the more chance you have of marrying a fabulous man. Become proficient in subjects such as skiing, history, art, philosophy, tennis, cooking, chess, and current events. The more you achieve, the more confidence you'll have.

Believe in yourself. Remember 19th-century novelist Anthony Trollope's advice: "And above all things, never think you are not good enough. ...never think that. My belief is that in life people will take you at your own reckoning."

Reinvent Yourself

If life hasn't always dealt you a great hand, why not start over? Reinvent yourself! Novelist George Eliot is said to have advised, "It's never too late to become the person you want to become." There are so many opportunities in life waiting for you, why not grab one? If it's hard to get going, try motivating yourself with the old adage, "If you don't start 'til you know the way, you'll never stir 'til Judgment Day."

I've known awkward 30-year-old ugly ducklings who glided into their forties as glamorous and formidable swans.

At age 33 Emily had been a hard-driving union activist, a real no-nonsense gal. She was smart and powerful, but I never heard anyone say she was attractive. We lost touch, but after 10 years passed, I saw her across the room at a party. She was almost unrecognizable. Emily had become a high-end interior decorator imbued with every ounce of elegance that went along with her profession. I elbowed my way past the men who were vying for her attention and whispered, "What happened? You're magnificent!"

She gave me an appreciative smile and answered, "I always wanted to live a glamorous life, so I decided to do something about it. I went back to school, pored through books and magazines, signed up at the gym, and got advice from beauty experts. No matter what happened I always kept one eye on my goals."

Are you like Emily, a beautiful butterfly trapped in a cocoon? Put in the time, do the work, and make the changes. Get a new job, move to a different city, or become a redhead. A more exciting you is waiting!

Educate Yourself

In today's world men are searching for accomplished women. Business magazines have claimed, "The new trophy wife went to Harvard Business School."

Men look at the superficial first, such as a woman's appearance, and then whether she's personable. But after that, they concentrate on the substantial. They ask themselves, "Does she have a good character? Does she have depth?" An old Russian proverb suggests, "A man wants to start the relationship because of your face, but he wants to continue the relationship because of your mind."

Men often ask me to introduce them to women in the scientific or medical professions. Female physicians are often viewed as angels of mercy. They seem to exude a nurturing image that doesn't interfere with a man's ego. I'm not sure why, but women in scientific fields seem to have fewer problems with gender competition.

Prospective bridegrooms want it all—a good body and a good mind. If a man isn't physically attracted to you, you may not get to first base. On the other hand if he doesn't respect you, you won't hit any home runs. It's easier to knock it out of the ballpark if you have a good education. If you don't, sign up for a class, even if it's on the Internet. Men appreciate women who want to continue learning, regardless of the subject.

Forgive Yourself

All of us, at one time or another, have said or done things we wish we hadn't. Sometimes it's almost too embarrassing to even think about. Why not forgive yourself?

I worked with a young Ivy League woman who is now broadcasting the news on CNN. Let's call her Annie. We met when Annie was just 23. Even then, she had the "forgive yourself" thing down. She'd write her transgressions on little pieces of paper and make a ceremony out of destroying each one while forgiving herself at the same moment.

Annie claimed this doesn't work unless you shred the paper and then either drown, bury, or burn it. She believed it helped her not to think about it again. She completely absolved herself.

Everything Annie touches turns to gold. I don't know where she ever got the idea about forgiving herself, but it works well. Along with making a meteoric rise to the top of her profession, Annie managed to find a remarkably wonderful husband. She is still one of the most mentally healthy women I know.

"If you want to get married, cook him his favorite meal."

—Esta, Pari's Italian seamstress

I'm sure some kindly older woman along the way probably advised you, "The way to a man's heart is through his stomach." When the man you're looking for was growing up, his mother was probably of the generation of women who raised sons to think that food was love. Cooking was a way to nurture families. This isn't always the case today.

Prospective brides should be able to prepare at least one or two simple and delicious meals. One tall, handsome man I know, who started his own airline, claims he finally decided to marry the woman I introduced him to after she prepared a standing rib roast and all of the trimmings for a group of his friends.

Take a cooking class or ask your friends who are marvelous cooks for suggestions. You can make some very tasty meals with only three or four ingredients.

But please, don't ever make a man a meal, or even offer to, until you've dated him several months. Do it after he's taken you to movies, plays, and several nice restaurants. Remember, you're setting a precedent for your whole relationship. And many working women today don't have the time or energy to cook a gourmet meal every night.

Instead, many men enjoy doing the cooking in today's world. Bon appétit!

Don't Be a Nurse or a Purse for Him

Try dating some older men. Also try dating some younger ones. The older ones may want to show you off to their friends. The younger ones may not want to introduce you to anyone. There are good things to be said about men of any age. Be open-minded enough to learn the good and bad. Just watch out for those "booty calls," when he calls you up around 10 p.m. and asks, "Can I come over?" Always have plans, company, or an early morning meeting at work that prevents you from seeing him. Saying yes to calls like these shows you don't have anything going on without him and that you're at his beck and call.

Run From the Rude Man

Was a man rude to you in a social setting? Don't make a fuss. Be kind and sweet. He'll probably feel guilty and regret his behavior. If you're clever enough, you can get in a cheerful bon mot. Zap him with sunshine. If you do this you'll be admired by everyone within earshot, especially the offender. The man will feel like a heel, and time wounds all heels. This technique works in business as well. If a man asks your age, how many times you've been married, or if you dye your hair, say, "Only my closest friends know, and maybe you will too one day."

"Power is the ultimate aphrodisiac."

—Henry Kissinger, former U.S. Secretary of State

Once in awhile a prince of a man will come along whose accomplishments will leave you breathless. If you would love to squeeze your foot into that glass slipper, but there's simply no magic, don't be so quick to turn into a pumpkin.

Take Janet, a popular restaurateur who found herself in just such a situation. Initially she was convinced her relationship with the man she called "Mr. Powerhouse" would never work. She just wasn't "into" him. But she continued to accept his invitations because he made her laugh and she admired his accomplishments. Each time they had dinner, she enjoyed him more. Janet admired his brilliant mind and his quiet confidence. Best of all he treated her like a queen. After only a few months, I was amazed when she proclaimed, "He has a body like Michelangelo's David and the brain of Einstein."

Janet and "Mr. Powerhouse" were married within the year and are still living happily ever after. She and I often giggle about the fairy tale life she almost missed.

Over time love can grow. If you admire a man but you're not sure about the fire in your heart, wait and see what happens. If you try for a while and the sparks still aren't there, then let some other Cinderella have a try.

"Never trust a woman who will give you her age. A woman who tells you that would tell you anything."

—Oscar Wilde, *writer*

If you are a wee bit older but still look terrific, why tell anyone your age? I'm not recommending that you lie; just don't give out that bit of information. It works best if you make a joke out of not disclosing it; just make it clear that you don't tell your age.

If He Thinks You're Younger and Sexier, Why Disillusion Him?

I know a man who never knew his wife's age until he read it on her tombstone. She had a don't ask, don't tell policy. He thought it was hilarious. During the course of their marriage when several people offered to reveal her secret, he wouldn't let them. He thought not knowing was too much fun and great material for cocktail parties. Isn't it all in the presentation?

When a man gets a little older, he likes to think he's still attractive to younger, sexier women. If he thinks you're younger and sexier, don't disillusion him. As long as he's not expecting to have children, what difference does it make?

"Never try to teach a pig to sing. It's a waste of your time, and you'll just irritate the pig." —Neil Evans, psychologist

Don't try to change anyone. If you're thinking about marrying the man, you must accept him for all of his assets and liabilities. The worst thing you can do is go into a relationship thinking you can change him. Actress Natalie Wood once said, "The only time a woman really succeeds in changing a man is when he is a baby." Don't whine, criticize, or nag. If you can't live with your man's faults, maybe it's time to part company.

"If you don't have something good to say about someone, don't say anything." —Thumper, from the movie Bambi

Although some men are bigger gossips than some women, don't let your man catch you gossiping. The gossip will either bore him or he'll think you're too catty. Your lover may be proud of you if you won't dish the dirt.

Some gossips are foolish enough to think the unkind things they say won't come back around and cause hurt feelings. If you make a lot of enemies, there's a big chance someone might start whispering about you. If your man hears you gossiping, it might make him wonder what you'd say about him and whether you'd make him a trustworthy wife.

It's easy to score points and seem funny when you make a biting comment about someone else. But be careful. Think about the long-term impact of what you say and apply the golden rule.

Love Me, Love My Kitty

Connie, a dental assistant with a big personality, lives with four cats, two dogs, and a parrot. Most of her male friends think she lives in a menagerie. One otherwise enthusiastic young man told me he couldn't date her because he didn't want to rank eighth on her list. "I want a woman who pays a lot of attention to me," he explained.

Although walking your dog can be a great way to meet a guy, it will scare some men away if your canine has a wardrobe that rivals your own or more than one box of dog toys. One poor fellow complained he reached for some savory looking morsel in a glass bowl on his date's coffee table and choked on her dog's treats.

Sandy, a gorgeous part-time student and part-time flight attendant, had a waist like a wasp. Most of the men I introduced her to adored her but confided that most of her conversations were about a horse she called "Bill." One night my roommate and I met Greg, a handsome rancher from Southern California. He spent all evening talking about his horse. We introduced Greg and Sandy and they fell deeply in love. Their wedding was the talk of the town. Sandy wore an old-fashioned *Girl of the Golden West* gown and Greg wore his best roundup clothes. The last time I spoke to Sandy and Greg, Bill had reached the ripe old age of 25 and had been let out to pasture.

Not all such stories have happy endings. If you have more than two animals, don't let the man you date feel neglected. Furry friends can ruin potential relationships. If your man has allergies or if he likes to travel, Rover or Gigi can cramp his style.

"*A man's love is mighty. He will even buy a nightie for a girl who he thinks is fun. But they don't buy pajamas for pistol-packing mamas. Oh, you can't get a man with a gun!*"

—from the musical Annie Get Your Gun

A woman shouldn't appear to be a rodeo wrangler roping a poor defenseless calf. If you're the aggressive type, skip the hard sell and relax! Unless the guy pursues you, he might think you're trying to change him from a raging bull to an emasculated steer. If he thinks you have him in your gun sights, he'll probably lose interest.

Do you think being too aggressive is one of your problems? Take the advice of a popular San Francisco socialite who cured her "I like to chase men" attitude with a thin silver bracelet. She called it her "Silver Silencer." She wore it to remind herself to let men go after her. Each time she found herself wanting to pursue a man, she would redirect her energy and play with her bracelet.

Fourteen months after she purchased the bracelet, she was married. Her husband replaced it with an emerald and diamond one, but she claims her Silver Silencer will always be her favorite piece of jewelry.

Bette Davis had something to say about pursuing men: "Men don't like to feel you're looking to catch them. If they feel that, they are likely to ride away." Bette wasn't exactly lucky in love, but she was married three times and knew something about getting those cowboys to propose.

> *"Success in life is more than finding the right person. Being the right person is even more important."* —Elof G. Nelson, *author*

Whenever I observe a woman who seems to be looking better than ever and has finally landed her dream job, I sit up and take notice. I know it won't be too long before she falls in love and gets married. The magic usually happens when a woman takes control of her life. Then she takes on a new aura. How much is luck? I've always believed the advice my dad gave me, "Luck is opportunity meeting preparation." If you make yourself the best person you can be, potential husbands will be coming out of the woodwork.

Take the case of Margaret, a paralegal, who wasn't meeting anyone. She eventually made a decision to get serious about her career and

go to law school. After she graduated she bought a new wardrobe and got a wonderful job. Margaret just glowed. It didn't surprise me when I received a phone call about her engagement to the CEO of a Fortune 500 company. When I questioned her about the wedding plans, she beamed, "He's paying for everything!" She asked him about the budget, and he said, "There is none. This is your special day. I want you to have what you want."

Ban Those Bad Boys

He may be smooth, sexy, and charismatic, but if you're dating a desperado, he may also be lyin', cheatin', and stealin' hearts. The only women who lasso these outlaws are holding high cards and playing a pretty mean game themselves.

Don't gamble if you've got a losing hand. If your guy is interested only in getting lucky and he doesn't treat you with respect, tell him to put his gun back in its holster and walk away. If he's always late, flirts outrageously with the waitress, or compares you unfavorably to his last girlfriend, send that bronco back to the corral.

After the Rain Comes the Rainbow

Every relationship has some troubled times. When the sun isn't shining, try to concentrate on his good points and appreciate the memorable times the two of you have shared. When one of the wisest women I know was asked about the secret of her happy relationship, she answered, "You have to let each other have your grumpy days." If you have to endure a few grumpy days and a few disappointments along the way, remember the wonderfully glorious things that made you fall in love with him in the first place. Keep your eye on the rainbow and savor the golden moments you spend with the man you love. Be the woman he wants to spend his life with, rain or shine.

"I'm seventy years old and there aren't too many rides left on the merry-go-round."

—Annabelle Johnson, physician and one of Pari's successful matches

A beautiful woman in her twenties can meet a man walking to the mailbox. As time goes on women used to getting attention from men report that between age 40 and 50 they begin to feel invisible. Don't let this discourage you. You can date older men and still feel adored. How much older is older? A decade or two makes less and less difference the older you get.

It's never too late for romance.

Many women enjoy an active love life well into their sixties, seventies, and beyond. I enjoyed matchmaking a stunning woman in her eighties who turned out to be quite a heartbreaker. If you want to be a sexy senior citizen, here are some great tips.

- **Men admire happy women.** Save the whine. Lead with your pleasures in life and a man will take pleasure in you.

- **Get out and enjoy yourself!** Stay active and continue learning.

- **Don't be too picky.** Broaden your field. Be flexible.

- **Earn your friends' husbands respect.** Widowed men often look to their wives' old friends for solace. Joan, a Long Island widow with a successful business, married three successive widowers. She outlived two of them and is still married to a third. Jealous rivals claimed that immediately after the death of each wife, Joan began sending the widower flowers and casseroles. Her romances seemed to begin on the funeral parlor steps. Her secret? All the men knew her well and admired her so much that when she expressed an interest, they couldn't resist.

- **Don't admit your age** and work hard to stay out of the larger sizes. One of the pleasures of living today is that no one has to feel stereotyped by age. The best is yet to come!

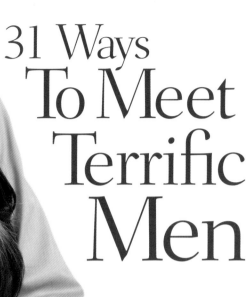

31 Ways To Meet Terrific Men

Try New Actions

1. Give a party with a man who has some great friends. You invite the women—he invites the men.

2. Practice recycling. Trade your old beaus with your friends.

3. Ask 10 friends you admire to introduce you to someone special.

4. Attend events with beautiful women. They'll make you sparkle too. Men flock to them and you can enjoy the overflow.

5. Matchmake your friends. Make sure they reciprocate.

6. Attend parties even if you don't feel like it. Many women who went to parties not counting on much found men they married.

7. Gravitate toward the hot spots at a party. Stand next to the group of people who look like they are having the best time.

8. Be friendly at your grocery store. If a man hovers around the pasta, give him your grandmother's recipe for tomato sauce.

9. If a guy has cool friends, throw him a surprise birthday party.

10. Donate time to nonprofit organizations in your community.

11. Join every organization that interests you.

12. Sign up with an Internet dating service. Try niche ones for people with similar interests such as religion, politics, or the arts.

13. Observe or participate in athletic events. Join a ski, volleyball, or tennis club.

14. Take a night class. Choose a subject you're interested in that you think would also appeal to someone with lots of testosterone.

15. Do a little flirting if you're in a safe environment. Don't be afraid to stare at an attractive man from across the room.

16. Offer your services to an election campaign or political group. Most men love politics.

17. Attend your house of worship. Take part in their events. If they don't have a singles group, offer to start one.

18. Host a salon. Invite artists to display their work and performers to perform in your home. Invite their friends.

19. Buy a dress that makes you feel beautiful and wear it often.

20. Learn to cook a few simple, delicious meals. Start a cooking class for singles.

21. Always try to look your best when you leave home. You never know when or where you'll meet someone.

Change Your Attitude

22. Understand what you want. List the three most important qualities you admire in a man. Only date men who have those qualities.

23. Be open-minded. If a man has the qualities you want, even if he's not perfect, make an effort to date outside your comfort zone.

24. Polish the facets of your life, both skills and attitudes.

25. Write your own commercial. List 10 things that are wonderful about you.

26. Forgive yourself.

27. Become an expert on a subject that interests you.

28. Reinvent yourself. Lose some weight, buy a new wardrobe, develop new interests, or break old habits.

29. Be positive, put on a happy face, and don't gossip.

30. Don't be too aggressive. Why serve yourself to a man on a silver platter? Make it more difficult; give him the can and let him open it.

31. Visualize a successful courtship and a beautiful marriage.

set:
How to Finetune
Your Dating
Skills

Find the good and
Praise it.

— Alex Haley, author

Tell your sweetheart what you love about him. No man can resist the phrase, "Do you know what my favorite thing is about you?" Or, "One of the reasons I admire you is -----." Never skip a chance to make the man you love feel bigger, better, and more important.

Cynthia was a great believer in praising people every time she had a sincere opportunity. She had a warm personality and long thick red hair. Her friends said she was easy to be around. Cynthia was sure her greatest assets were her ability to get along with people and her printing company, which she had nurtured for years.

Her big break came when a handsome, brilliant man they called "The Wiz of Wall Street" hired her to do some printing for his company. Serendipitously he also invited her to lunch. After their first meeting each time they met she praised him about his character and his many accomplishments. He was a little standoffish at first, but she won him over. Eventually he became

responsive to her. After 18 months they were in London on a holiday and decided to elope. When they returned to the United States, he told all his coworkers, "Cynthia thinks I'm better than I am—she brings out the best in me."

Make Him Laugh

If you can amuse him, I'm betting on you! If you can laugh together...great peals of laughter until your sides hurt...if his personality just tickles you or if he thinks your antics are adorable—back that horse. You just hit the Triple Crown. The odds are humor can help you make a run for the roses and there'll be a lovely photo finish on your wedding day.

Surprise Him

Rudyard Kipling's poem "The Ladies" has bittersweet moments:

I have taken my fun where I've found it,

But now I must pay for my fun,

For the more you have seen of the many,

The less you will cling to the one.

Don't be just one woman—be two, three, or even four different women. I'm not suggesting you develop a multiple personality disorder, but we all have several sides to ourselves. Just when he thinks you're soft and feminine, be a little naughty. When he's convinced you're a little naughty, become sleek and elegant. Do it effortlessly, not frenetically, and never be boring. If he thinks you're a great golfer, demonstrate you can also make a great red velvet cake. Show him all your different skills and all the various sides of your personality. Do a little marketing. Surprise him with the dynamic you!

Don't Give Away Your Power

If you've started to date someone and he says he'll call you on Monday, but he doesn't, don't mention it. If you do he'll realize how much you care for him and you'll lose all your power. Date other men and you won't care if he calls you on Monday. Somebody else will.

Don't ask a man if he's interested in you or in having a relationship. Don't demand more of his time. Do these and you'll lose your power. He'll believe you're smitten and he has got you on the hook. Never worry if your man cares about you. Worry if you care about him.

Some men are like Groucho Marx, who said he didn't want to belong to a club that would have him as a member. A man likes to strive to win a woman's attention.

The more difficult the task, the more desirable the woman. Think of Greek mythology. Men competed fiercely for Helen of Troy. Understand that if you do all the worrying, you take away his fun.

Research indicates that men are biologically programmed to do the chasing. It's a ritual that has been going on since Adam and Eve.

Just like birds and animals, humans have a little mating dance. Enjoy it, have fun, but don't give away your power. Remember, in nature it's the female that ultimately does the choosing.

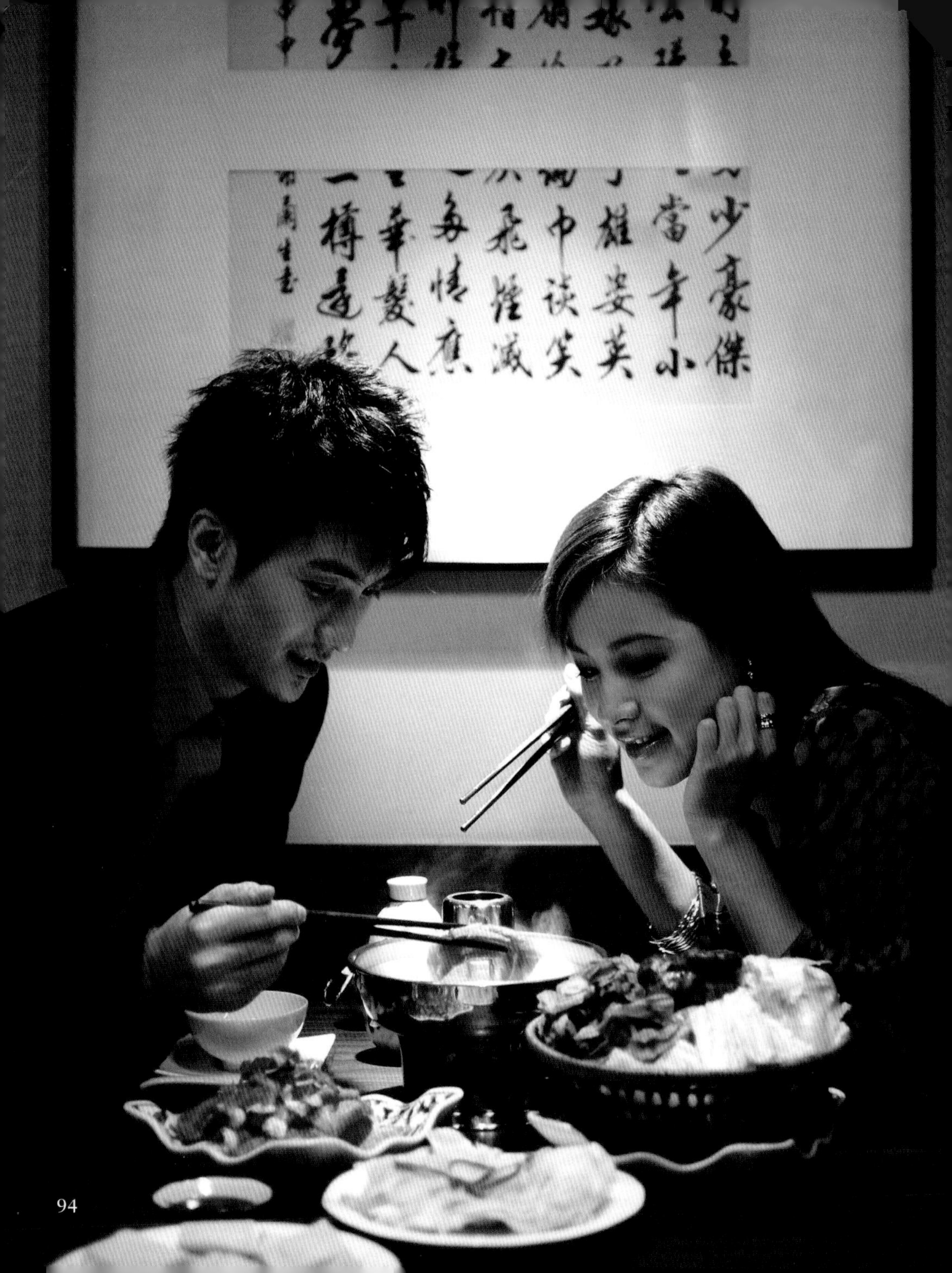

If He Invites You, He Treats You. If You Invite Him, You Treat Him.

If a man asks you out for the evening, keep your hands in your pockets when the dinner bill comes. Don't offer to pay your share. If he invites you he should pay the freight. If he continually pays for your meals and entertainment, however, you should reciprocate. My suggestions include:

- home-cooked meals

- concert tickets

- tickets to his favorite athletic events

- movie passes.

If you date long term, you can reciprocate a little more generously. If you suggest an outing, you should always pay the bill.

Chemistry Is Not Negotiable

If you're dating a man who is absolutely perfect on paper but doesn't knock your socks off, turn him into a friend. A man's ego is delicate, so be diplomatic. If you're unsure how to do it, try saying, "Although we admire each other very much, I'm sure it's obvious to the two of us that we don't have much chemistry." Or, "I think we both agree that we are probably going to end up as platonic friends." Help him to understand that you aren't rejecting him.

If you've given it the old college try and he doesn't make your toes curl, it won't work. You can have a terrific relationship, but when the going gets tough, sex and physical attraction are the glue that holds a relationship together.

Pearls of Wisdom

If you understand what kind of man you want, but you've never had a relationship with that kind of man or that type of person hasn't asked you out in years, it's time to compromise.

Does he really need to be so handsome, so smart, or so charming? Natalie, the head nurse at a hospital, was 41 and disappointed she had no husband and no family. Although she's lovely she had a long list of nonnegotiable expectations. I suggested she think about which two or three qualities were most important to her and then begin dating with an open heart.

Almost immediately I introduced her to a wonderful man who also longed for a family. It didn't take them long to fall in love. Last summer she and her husband hosted a birthday celebration for their 2-year-old twin boys.

If you're having problems connecting, have a heart-to-heart talk with yourself. Keep an open mind about things that really don't matter and search for a man with a sterling character and a heart of gold. If you start concentrating on his insides and not his outsides, you might meet a diamond in the rough. What fun you could have polishing him!

Help Him Believe in Himself

If you want to spend the rest of your life with a man, it's your job to make him feel important and well loved. He should understand that you admire him and he should understand why. If you accomplish this he'll always look forward to seeing you. And if you can help him believe in himself, he'll always believe in you.

If you tell a man you admire him because he has an outstanding character and give him examples why, he'll always want to do his best to be a man of true integrity. If you tell him you admire his manners, no matter how top-notch they already are, you will notice an improvement. Just as he tried to please his mother, he will try to please you. In some sweet ways they're all little boys after all.

Be the Flame, Not the Moth

Some women love to be the aggressors. If men appear to be disinterested, these gals are anxious to pursue them. Talk about getting your wings singed: Sierra, a gorgeous investment banker educated at Yale, is interested in men only when they run away from her. She confided, "I just keep chasing them until I've made such a fool of myself, I can't bear to ever see them again."

I guess that's one way to handle it, but it certainly isn't good for your reputation or your emotional health. "When they're hot, they're hot, and when they're not, they're not." If you think you're going to get burned, blow that candle out and find someone who thinks you are the flame.

Never tell men you want to get married and have babies—they'll run like rabbits

When you first start dating, if you want to get married and have a baby, don't mention it—that's not being honest, it's being stupid. Most men have an ego the size of Texas, and if you even mention the word marriage they'll consider it a proposal. Pipe down on the baby, baby!

Turn the question around. If a man asks you if you want to get married, be sweet, but say something like, "Please understand, I've had some dates lately with men who only want to talk about marriage. I have to be very forthright and let you know I'm not interested in rushing into a permanent relationship. I do enjoy your company, however, and I like you a little more each time we meet. But let's go slowly." That will put things in the right perspective. Men love to do the chasing. Let them.

Watch How He Treats His Mother

Is he kind and considerate to his family? Then he'll probably be kind and considerate to yours. Pay particular attention to the way he treats his mother. She set the pattern for his relationships with women. If he does not respect her, he may not respect you.

Watch out for unresolved conflicts. Many men marry women who remind them of their mothers. If a man has had a strong, intelligent, and independent mother, he will probably not need to control you.

Some men are still trying to please their mothers, which often translates to women who are their love interests. This isn't all bad. A man may look to you for affirmation and affection. If you unselfishly give it to him, he could be yours for life.

"Some of us are becoming the men we wanted to marry."

—Gloria Steinem, author and speaker

Women are learning they can become whatever they want to become. My favorite female CEO told me that, for her, getting married only led to doing housework.

If you have many interests and are independent emotionally and financially, don't overlook your options. Marriage may not be right for you. There is nothing wrong with having a guy in every port: one man to take you to baseball games and another to take you to the opera; one to discuss business opportunities and another to cook dinner for you.

Depending on their lifestyles some women are much happier living single. Remember, you can have the best of all possible worlds if you marry the right man or the worst of all possible worlds if you marry the wrong one. Or you may choose not to marry at all.

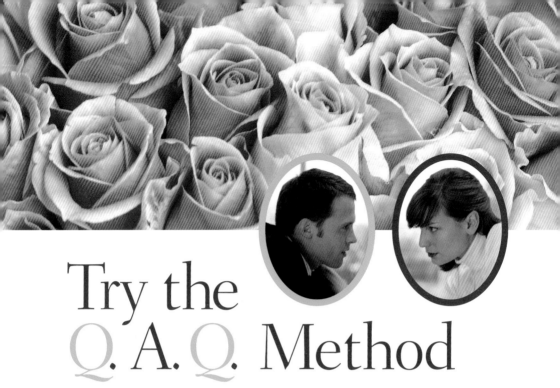

Try the
Q. A. Q. Method

Some of the most exciting men I know have complained to me, "She talked about herself all evening and never asked me one question." Such women think the first date is meant for advertisement and not for conversation.

Some of these women want to be certain their dates understand why they are so special. Other such women are just a little nervous and will chatter about anything to fill in the breaks in the conversation. Some are just salespeople.

Men want to impress you, particularly on first dates. Give them the chance to talk about their favorite subject: themselves. If you ask enough questions, you will have a better opportunity to evaluate your feelings about the man you are dating. You will also have a better chance to understand his good and bad qualities. Men will be more impressed with you if you are sincerely interested in them.

Even if you go out with a man who spends most of the evening asking you questions, employ the Q.A.Q. (Question, Answer, Question) Method. Here are two examples of how it works:

MAN QUESTION: You mentioned you play tennis. How often do you play?

WOMAN ANSWER: I play about once or twice a week. But I'd rather find out about you. WOMAN QUESTION: Which sports do you enjoy?

MAN QUESTION: So, you're an investment analyst. Do you like your job?

WOMAN ANSWER: Yes, I do. But I'm much more interested in what you do. I'd love to hear about how you started your investment firm. It sounds so impressive. WOMAN QUESTION: Will you please tell me about it?

Women who use the Q.A.Q. method become much more successful at evaluating the men they date. It's eye-opening and a timesaver. As for the men they date, they find the clever women who use Q.A.Q. to be absolutely charming!

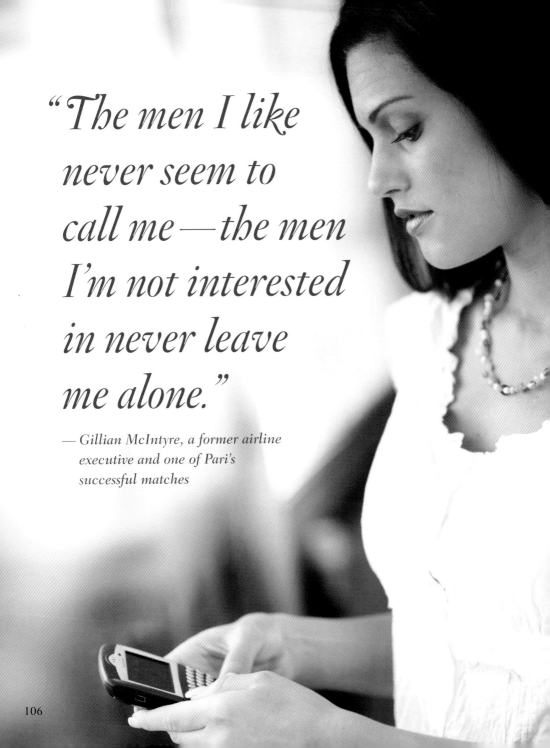

"The men I like never seem to call me —the men I'm not interested in never leave me alone."

— Gillian McIntyre, a former airline executive and one of Pari's successful matches

For some women the most difficult thing about dating is learning how to say no. Every woman has received calls from men to whom they have no particular attraction. If a fellow seems interesting, by all means give him a try. But if you find yourself wanting to press an eject button that will take you home to that favorite chair in your living room, learn how to field those unwanted calls.

The always popular and exceedingly correct Miss Manners gives some worthwhile advice: "If you don't wish to go out with a man, simply say, 'I'm sorry, I just can't.'" It's not necessary to explain why.

If you tell a gentleman you won't be able to see him because your favorite aunt is ill or you just twisted your ankle on the living room carpet, you risk getting caught. Why perjure yourself? Simply tell him you are sorry but you can't go. After you do that two or three times, he'll eventually get the hint.

Of course, if it's a man who really interests you, don't let him get away. If you have plans on the day he suggests and you would love to spend some time with him, always offer an alternative date.

Quick tip: If a man has some redeemable qualities, but he's not for you, introduce him to someone more appropriate. Be flattering. This will cushion the blow, and your matchmaking will gain points with him. One of your friends may find him very desirable.

"Thank You For Dinner" Is Enough

Dating etiquette still stands. If a man takes you out for a fabulous evening, you don't owe him anything. He's not entitled to a good night kiss or a quick squeeze in the taxi. If you are having a wonderful time, kiss him if you'd like. It's not your obligation! You can show your appreciation in words and lavish phrases. If you mention specifics, "The dill sauce was fabulous" or "I loved Matt Damon in that movie," it'll have more of an impact.

However don't send a thank-you note for a nice dinner. He may consider it a plea for attention. Telephone calls, emails, and letters to "thank him for the lovely evening" always build a man's ego, but they're unnecessary and may leave him thinking, "I guess she really likes me, so now who's next?"

A Kiss Is Still A Kiss

The scientific name for kissing is philematology. Men love philematology! It leads to things they like even better.

Kiss your man often and wholeheartedly—not just on the lips. Kiss his forehead while he reads the newspaper or kiss his ear while you lightly nibble on it. And here's good news for dieters: If you kiss someone passionately for five minutes, you'll burn 130 calories. Maybe that's why falling in love is so good for the waistline. If you'd like to lose some weight, why not KISS IT OFF?

Leave the Past In the Past

Don't discuss your previous relationships, particularly not ex-husbands. If you date a man long enough, he'll ask you about your old flames. Find some charming or humorous way to divert the subject. Say something like, "Joe and I have a deal. I don't say anything bad about him, and he doesn't say anything bad about me." Or plead, "I don't like to dwell on the past. I prefer to concentrate on today and tomorrow." Don't bad-mouth the men in your past and your new friends will admire you for it.

Many men will try to pressure you for information about your former lovers. Some do it to see how they measure up. If you confess that

the last three men you dated were losers, your current lover may wonder how he wound up in such inferior company.

If you must discuss the men in your past, don't talk about your broken heart; talk about the hearts you've broken. If you talk too much about your last relationship, new men you meet will not believe you are ready for another. Divulge minimal information. It's easy to get caught in the trap of discussing old loves and before you know it, the evening is about to end and you and your date know very little about one another. After that kind of evening, men rarely ask for an encore.

Be an
Expert

A single woman should always strive to become an expert in at least one subject. It's better if it's something the man you are dating knows very little about. Knowledge about topics with which he is unfamiliar will make an impression.

If you don't feel knowledgeable about subjects that might interest men, do research. The man you're dating should understand that you're very well versed about this topic. But don't lay it on so thick that he thinks it's all you want to talk about.

Choose a subject that really interests you. It can be almost anything: wine, Turkish rugs, dog breeds, or even biotechnology.

Read magazines and search the Internet. Memorize facts and figures. Put time into it. If you don't, you won't be an expert and won't be credible. Being a phony is a lot worse than being an airhead. Whatever happens with that guy, you'll learn and grow.

When a man is in love, he enjoys bragging about the woman he dates. In today's world it is important that he be able to appreciate your intellectual capabilities.

Becoming an expert will also make you popular at dinner parties. Learn to bring every conversation around to your favorite topic.

When you're informed about a subject and you accomplish your goal, you'll be happier with yourself. The more accomplishments you achieve, the more confidence you'll have. A self-confident woman is always more interesting to a man.

If He Says He's Not Good Enough for You, He May Be Right

I dentify what's true! It is ok to turn a blind eye to the awkward mistakes a man makes while you are dating, but the minute you discover he has a flawed character, don't continue to see him. Never mind that a lot of romantic novels say, "The love of a good woman will save him." That's a myth!

Your most ardent dream should be to find a man with integrity. Sometimes it takes a long time for a woman to realize that good looks, confidence, and a nice butt are not the most important qualities in a man.

If you have a man with good character, you have everything.

"The less they know, the better they sleep."

— *Irina Cordell, former makeup artist and one of Pari's successful matches*

Trust and respect are the foundations of a good relationship. For this reason never lie to your man. But don't tell him everything. Skip the parts about family problems, your last boyfriend, or your last 15 parking tickets. Your brother's four divorces or your mother's nervous breakdown are also not desirable topics. Bathe yourself in the best light possible and don't volunteer unflattering information. Whenever you confide in a man, ask yourself, "Is what I'm about to say kind? Is it truthful? And is it necessary?" Answer his questions truthfully. But remember, a little mystery is better than lots of negative information.

Beware the
Braggart

Some men go from outright bragging to outright lying. If they're deceitful about little things, they'll probably be deceitful about bigger ones. Before you get roped in, if something sounds too good to be true, check the facts. Keep your eyes open and ask lots of questions.

Beverly, a manicurist from San Jose, went out with a real estate developer named Sam from San Francisco for about four months. He claimed he had another home in Houston and still another in Bar Harbor, Maine. Although he had a Honda parked at his home in San Jose, he said he drove his Jaguar in longhorn country and his Range Rover in the Pine Tree State.

Beverly discovered his friends had no knowledge of his other homes or other automobiles. She finally told Sam she was going to Houston and would love to spend some time with him and his Jaguar when she was in town. She never heard from him again.

If you think the man you are dating is lying to you, don't continue your relationship. Lies may also include lies of omission. The last time I saw Beverly she told me if she ever spoke to Sam again and he said it was raining, she'd go to the window and check. In good and bad weather, you need a boat that sails true.

Use the
Rule of
Three

Use this winning technique only after you've gone out for at least a month with your new flame and think you may have a future with him. You should have hobbies and interests in common, enjoy his company, and find him a quality person. If he cheats his best friend, flirts with the waitress, or never visits his mother, don't use it. You'll be sorry.

Here's how it works. Note each time he asks you out and decline every third time. Make it friendly, positive, and upbeat. Tell him, "I'd love to, but I have plans." Never tell what plans. Be lighthearted. If he asks who you're seeing, say, "Just friends." Don't say you have a date or hint that you do.

Of course your plans could be bathing your shih tzu. (But you'd be seeing a friend, wouldn't you?) Or you could be cozying up to *Sex and the City* reruns in your furry pink bathrobe with some friendly malted milk balls. Don't explain. Later if he asks if you had a good time, say yes and change the subject.

Men love mystery. They also love not to be completely sure of you, especially at the beginning. A woman who is a bit reticent presents an enigma, a puzzle waiting to be put together, a sonnet not quite written, a song with the last stanzas not yet composed. Resist the urge to tell all.

And that includes clueing him in on the rule of three, should you two tie the knot.

Celebrate!

Always make holidays special. The gifts you buy for him should be thoughtful, yet not too expensive. Don't overdo it: It upsets the balance of the relationship. If you're seeing a man exclusively, never forget his birthday. Make a tradition of Christmas, Hanukkah, Kwanzaa, New Year's Eve, Valentine's Day, and Easter. Whichever holidays you and your man celebrate, observe them heartily. An enterprising woman I know makes red dinner on Valentine's Day and green dinner on St. Patrick's Day; her special man just loves it.

Create beautiful memories and you'll melt the heart of any man.

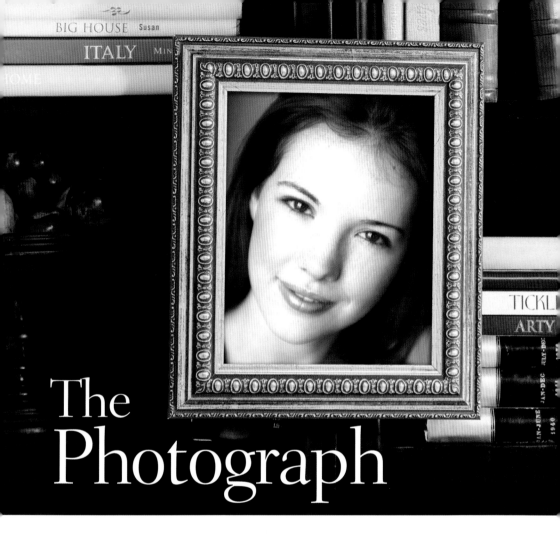

The Photograph

I f you're dating a man exclusively, always give him a smashing photograph of you, preferably a close-up shot. Present it in a fabulous frame he'll want to display so he can always be reminded of you. It's a great way to mark your territory. A wallet-size photo to accompany him is great for bragging about around the office or the gym.

Love Him, Love His Friends

Never say anything negative about his friends, his family, or his dog. Even if he detests his Uncle Charley, find something positive to say, such as "I'm sure he has some good points." He may not admit it, but he will secretly love you for saying it. Be especially nice to your sweetheart when you meet his friends. You can say something nice about anyone if you try. For example, about his best bud Max, who hogs the chip bowl and ignores utensils, say: "Max really has a good appetite." If his companions feel you make him happy, they'll be glad to accept you.

Getting to
"I Love You"

Don't say it first. Be patient and let him bring up the "L" word. If you've been waiting for four or five months and love is still not in his vocabulary, give him a little nudge. You might say, "I'm not sure, but I think I'm falling in love with you." If he's uncertain of his feelings, this is your clue to exit stage left. If he can't say "I love you," don't waste your time. If he can't use the "L" word, you'll never get to the "M" word.

Never Let a Man Pay Your Bills or You'll Become His Employee

Many wealthy men use their money to impress and control their women. If someone attempts such tactics with you, don't accept any scholarships. He may offer to pay your rent, give you a clothing allowance, or even buy you an expensive car. Tell that type of man to skip it. Suggest he bring flowers, books, or candy.

If you don't accept his expensive gifts, this will intrigue him. He's probably accustomed to buying whatever and whomever he wants. If his money won't influence you, he will have to become a man worthy of being with you. He will have to impress you with his time, effort, and personality. This man will realize you love him only for himself. On the other hand if you accept his lavish presents, he will believe you will not be around if he ever loses all his money. (This worries many men with large bank accounts.)

Accepting his offerings makes you a target for his manipulation. The more he gives you, the harder it will be to break away. He will believe it's enough to pay your bills and he won't have to marry you. If you get yourself a Sugar Daddy, you'd better ask for a nice watch. It may remind you not to waste your time.

I once told one of the wealthiest men in the country that it wasn't necessary to give a woman a diamond bracelet on the second or third date. He responded, "Don't you see what I'm doing? It saves me a lot of time. If she takes the jewelry, I know we're going right home to bed, no arguments. If she refuses I know I'm in for the long haul because she will be the kind of woman who really interests me. If I really like someone, it's worth the $10,000 or $15,000 it takes to filter her out."

He was a louse, but an exciting one. There are dozens of women floating around with lots of nice jewelry who found it hard to forget him.

Men who try to control women with their money are not happy when the gifts become the focus of their relationships. One Silicon Valley millionaire with an expensive girlfriend once told me, "It won't work. She's interviewing for mistress, but I'm interviewing for wife."

"Never allow your lover to see you do anything that is not alluring."

—Susan Wright Morris, one of Pari's successful matches

There is something to be said about keeping romance in a relationship. All of us are human, but if he thinks you're a goddess, try to keep that idea going for as long as possible. So, no green facial masks that make you look like an alien or eyebrow waxing. You're just naturally gorgeous. Right? Right.

"...a rose by any other name would smell as sweet."

—William Shakespeare

A study reported on CNN concluded that men were more attracted to women who wore the scent of grapefruit than any other aroma or perfume. Other aroma winners were pineapple and cinnamon. Grandmother might have been right: The way to a man's heart may very well be through his stomach.

If you would like to drive your man wild, answer the door wearing a grapefruit body soufflé and serve him a Greyhound (vodka and pink grapefruit juice) or a Pina Colada (pineapple juice, coconut cream, and light rum) before dinner. Fresh pineapple and grapefruit slices could be dessert.

If you want your man to be attracted by you, soak yourself in a scented bubble bath! But if you like scent, learn how to wear it:

- **Apply perfume in three squirts.** If you repeat the words "head, tummy, toes," it will help.

- **Don't wear scent to cover odors** you wish to hide.

- **Find out if the man you date** has objections or is allergic to perfume.

When you visit the cosmetic counter, try scents until you find one you like. It's less confusing if you experiment with one at a time. In general avoid heavy perfumes. You want your scent to whisper your essence, not shout it.

Don't Get Your Honey Where You Get Your Money

If you are serious about your career, don't link your name romantically with anyone in the office. Any promotion that you receive will be seen as a sexual trophy. You and everyone else will wonder if you really deserved it. A woman's worst nightmare should be picturing her office mates giggling around the watercooler about her sexual dalliances.

If you are dating the man you work for, don't jeopardize both your careers. Quit dating him or quit your job.

How to Mend Your Broken Heart

When a relationship falls apart, women handle it in different ways. Some hit the ground running and some go into deep mourning. If you're talking about divorce or death, they take much more time to get over than simply nursing a broken heart; allow yourself some time to recover and then focus on moving along:

- **Throw away all mementos** and photographs of him.

- **Put anything he's left** at your place in a box and mail it back.

- **Make a toast to the good times** with him and then break the glass.

The sooner you meet someone else, the sooner you'll feel better. Your broken heart will mend when you fall in love again. So don't be shy. Get out and try!

"If a relationship is going to work, you have to both be going at the same speed, in the same direction." —Kim Novak, actress

Timing is important. Both parties must be ready to make a commitment. Commonality is even more important. You must consider goals, interests, and temperaments:

- **If your goals are closely aligned** with your man's, your relationship will work better. If you haven't written your goals, try it. It's called values clarification. Here's how it works: On a piece of paper write three things you want to achieve. On the other side write three things you don't. Read it often to help you reach your goals.

- **Similarity of interests** builds strong bonds in a couple.

- **Closely observe a man's temperament** to determine if it's compatible with yours. Some people are merry-go-rounds and some people are roller coasters. Understand what you're dealing with before you go through the tunnel of love.

Boycott the
Bum's Rush

Some men want to talk about marriage almost immediately. At times "I love you" is a tactic rather than an emotion. Some men know what women want to hear and others are just in love with love itself. Listen to what the man says but say very little in return unless you're forced to. Just let him keep talking himself into becoming more deeply in love with you. If you're too eager it may

backfire. If he's not mature he may say to himself, "I've got her, now what?" And then he may become frightened and run away.

If you don't think he's the one, end the relationship. If you like him fasten your seat belt. This type of man could be the one your mother always warned you about. After a few months everything will become clear; in the meantime, enjoy the ride.

Wear One Hat in the Bedroom And Another in the Boardroom

Most men admire bright, accomplished women. If a man is interested in you, he will want to know all about your achievements. Provide him only with brief summaries because he will want to spend more time talking about himself. Don't do too much talking. Squeeze out your accomplishments like you would your toothpaste—just a little each night. If he falls in love with you, he will want to listen to every detail about your life. Save it for pillow talk.

The men you date are not looking for a competitive relationship. They prefer to compete with their colleagues and adversaries in the workplace. From you they will want nurturing, caring, and hugging. A minimum of four hugs a day is a great recipe for success.

Your man will also need you to respect him and to listen to him after a long day's work. It's your job to make him feel important. Emphasize your femininity. Help him enjoy the differences between men and women. Vive la difference!

On the other hand pay attention to whether or not he is curious about you. If he asks no questions or doesn't seem to care about what you do or think, watch out! That could be the recipe for the rest of your life and it's too hard to swallow.

Before You Measure Him For a Wedding Tux, See if He Measures Up

You owe it to yourself to ask him lots of questions. A man is flattered when a woman seems interested in what he has to say. Develop questions and subquestions about everything you would like to know about him. In particular, review the qualities you would like a man to have and think of questions you can ask to discover if he shares your values.

Don't divulge too much information about yourself. Let the man do most of the talking and he will think you are a brilliant conversationalist. Just listen. Don't feed him the answers and never let him think you might be judging him.

Don't let yourself fall in love with anyone until you have discovered everything you need to know about him. Experiment with different ways of determining his character, even if it takes months of conversation. Try to find out what you have in common. Promise yourself not to enter into a sexual relationship until you are sure he is right for you.

When a man introduces you to his friends and family, it becomes your privilege and responsibility to ask them questions about him. Use your charm and be smart about how you do it. Lots of women have ditched the men they were dating when family members provided some unflattering information.

Many women are so eager to fall in love that if an attractive man appears, they assign him qualities he doesn't really have. Don't gloss over his faults because you are overly eager to care about someone.

Remember the old Rodgers and Hart song, "Falling in love with love is falling for make-believe." Unless you ask the right questions, you may have to live with your trumped-up fantasies for the rest of your life.

Keep your feet on the ground, do your homework, and wait until you have all the necessary information before you allow yourself to become emotionally involved.

Learn How to Fight
In a Healthy Way

If you have a temper, develop some conflict management tools. When you have a disagreement, try to react in a cool and calm manner. Hysterics, yelling, and screaming won't get you anywhere. Proceed with kindness.

If your man really makes you angry, leave the room and go for a walk. Every man wants to think the woman he loves is a princess, but as Tom Arnold says, "Any man who thinks he's dating the princess, and doesn't realize he's also dating the wicked witch is in trouble."

The important thing is to learn how to fight. Stay away from men who are adrenalized by anger. A man who is turned on by anger is not worth your time and effort.

But no matter how much you love someone, there will always be times when you have disagreements. Every man has his weaknesses. If your guy isn't playing fair, you can make a few points that will quickly put him in his place. Be gentle, but get your point across.

Never allow him to criticize you in front of others. Take the advice of Sara, a gorgeous computer science professor who was dating Thomas, one of the Forbes 400. One weekend they were out to lunch with a few of his pals and he teased her about her figure right in front of them. Sara was mortified. When she got him alone, she said, "People are in relationships to support one another. If you ever do that again, I will leave and that will be the end of our relationship." He never criticized her again in front of others, and their large wedding was the social event of the season.

If your man tells you that you're not so perfect because you do this or that, you might try another good tactic. Say, "Well you're not so perfect either, but I love you unconditionally and I accept everything about you. I hope you will treat me in the same way."

7 Things You Really Need To Know About Sex

1. Making love is not a "getting-to-know-you" activity.

2. Make sure he deserves you! Ask the right questions before becoming involved. Sometimes women want to fall in love so much, they see qualities a man doesn't actually have.

3. Avoid disappointment. If you are seeing a man regularly it's a good rule to wait at least three months before becoming intimate.

4. The anticipation of having sex is very powerful. It may be to your advantage to hold on to that power just as long as you can.

5. Having sex changes your relationship—you lose your mystery. When the challenge is gone, making love can decrease his feelings for you and increase your feelings for him. You're less likely to be hurt if you're sure he's emotionally attached.

6. Never let yourself be drawn into arguments about having sex. Be clear about "no." But deliver it with charm and/or humor.

7. Don't travel with him unless you intend to sleep together. Even if he'll pay for separate rooms or if you pay for your own room, it's not worth the guilt trips and arguments that may go along with it.

Don't Let Him
Bug You

It's not a pretty topic, but there are some ugly and dangerous germs out there. Practice safe sex—protect yourself against sexually transmitted diseases. It's nonnegotiable!

Both partners should get tested before becoming sexually involved. Make it a bonding experience by getting tested together. The website www.cdc.gov/std will give you more information about sexually transmitted diseases.

Before a sexual encounter you and your potential lover should agree on a method of birth control. Condoms are a good choice.

The Older Dad

Some women are concerned about dating an older man because they fear he will not want to have children. It is important to determine his feelings about parenting fairly early in the relationship. Before sleeping with him, you may want to ask him if he has had a vasectomy. This would be a normal question a woman may ask to determine what type of birth control the couple will use. While you are on the subject, ask him if he has ever gotten a woman pregnant and how he would feel if it ever happened. Keep it general—do not ask what he would do if you got pregnant. If you want a child and it is clear he does not want children, look before you leap.

Don't be concerned that an older dad might not be a good father. Many men who have previously had children are much better parents the second time around. The first time they may have been busy fighting to get to the top and did not have time to concentrate on their little ones. Things can change, however. I often see older dads at parties who can't wait to get me in the corner and reach into their breast pocket for the latest photo of their little girl or boy. They often explain, "I'm a much better father than I ever was before. This is the best thing that has ever happened to me."

Dealing with Children

When you are in your twenties, you may not want to date men who have been divorced or have children. That policy makes everything a lot easier. As you age, however, you will discover that this is a young woman's privilege. By the time you hit your mid-thirties, it should become clear that if you refuse to date men who have never had children, the pickings get pretty slim. It is possible to meet such men, but it greatly diminishes the number of men who are available to you. If you are in your forties or above, such restrictions are "social suicide."

When dating men with children, try to realize that the laws of nature dictate you will probably come second to his kids. This is a difficult concept for some single women to accept, and men with kids often try to avoid women who have not had children.

If your latest flame is a package deal, try to be patient with him regarding his kids and ex-wife. He will probably have enough hassles already. Try not to become one of them.

I introduced Herb, a physician, to Martha, a marketing representative. He said he had divorced his ex-wife because every day she woke up fighting and he just couldn't take it anymore. Herb was so delighted to be involved with a woman who made his life so easy.

Some people think the ugliest word in the English language is stepmother. Fairy tales haven't helped this situation. When dealing with his children, if you intend to marry their father, always be a friend-type rather than a mother-type. Encourage him to do the necessary disciplining. The children will appreciate you if you praise their dad and never say anything negative about their mom.

Open your heart and you'll find that love comes in as many colors as crayons. One man and his children may ultimately not be right for you, but it is a wonderful practice to meet them and learn to appreciate without expectation.

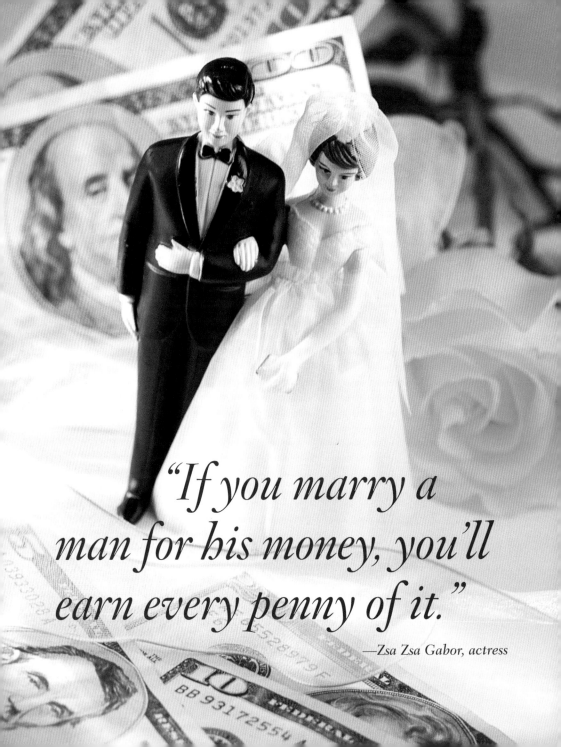

"If you marry a man for his money, you'll earn every penny of it."

—Zsa Zsa Gabor, actress

Living with a man you're not attracted to is hard work. Almost no one can stand it for very long.

I believe it occurs much less than people imagine it does. Even when it seems to you that a couple is a mismatch, there could be all kinds of dynamics that work for them that aren't obvious to the world.

When a man becomes your husband, he deserves your love, time, and affection. If you have to force yourself to give him what he deserves, it's a real jail sentence.

Love holds a relationship together. If you don't have love, you don't have anything. Diamonds may be a girl's best friend, but jewels, furs, and automobiles cannot replace the feeling of deeply caring about someone and being cared for in return. The acquisition of material goods will never make a hot-blooded woman truly happy. If cold, hard cash is your motivation, expect to be disappointed. Remember what Dolly Levi said in *Hello, Dolly!*: "If money is what's important, you can always snuggle up to your cash register. It's a little lumpy, but it rings!"

" You got to know when to hold 'em, know when to fold 'em. Know when to walk away and know when to run."

—Kenny Rogers, musician

Don't tolerate abusive behavior. He doesn't have to hit to hurt you. If he is verbally abusive, WALK AWAY. If he is physically abusive, don't try to change him. And don't give him another chance. RUN!

Make no exceptions! This is as much about preserving your self-esteem as your safety. If he is a substance abuser, don't turn a blind eye. Don't enable a man with abusive characteristics. A queen of hearts would think more highly of herself.

150

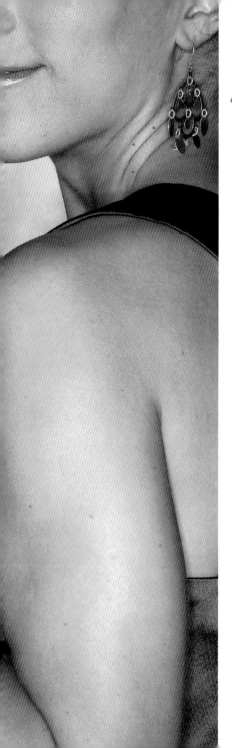

" If a man is too controlling, that's not caring; it's owning."

— Martha Richardsen,
   one of Pari's successful matches

Keep your independence. You can keep him too, if you can make him understand that women no longer want to be exclusively at the hearth and in the home. Our men find us more exciting, more interesting, and a lot happier if we are learning something, working toward accomplishments, and having experiences, which help us grow.

Let Him Down on The Satin Cushion

Smart women are rarely dumped. They are the ones who break up. They are the ones who end it.

I worked with a glamorous actress who confided, "The secret is to stay as long as you can when you're winning and quit as quickly as you can when you're losing." Have a little pride. You don't want him bragging all about how he's ditched you. Sometimes you'll break up with someone because you absolutely can't bear another evening with him. Sometimes you split because it isn't going anywhere. When you say goodbye, consider his feelings. Always let him down on a SATIN CUSHION. If you don't know what to say, the following methods work well:

- At the beginning of your relationship, claim you recently ended things with a fellow who meant a lot to you. Give no details. When it's time to unhitch say, "If I'd met you first, who knows what would have happened. I'm so sorry."

- Tell him your life is hectic now and you need a little break. Leave the door open. Let him know you might get back to him later.

- Tell him it's obvious both of you have concluded you aren't right for each other. (Make it sound mutual.) Suggest he'll be perfect for your marvelous friend. Be sincere—think of someone great.

- Leave a rose on his pillow. A stunning venture capitalist I work with is a real heartbreaker. When she stops dating a man, she sends him a book she knows he'll enjoy and encloses a flattering "Dear John" letter. Many of the fellows she has dropped have cried on my shoulder. I've nicknamed her the Book Bandit.

Getting out of a relationship when it's still early leaves loose ends. But if you're the one who ended things, you can pick up the threads again if you decide to weave your way back into the relationship, and he'll let you.

"If it's not going to work, there's nothing you can do to make it work. If it's going to work, there's nothing you can do to stop it." —Ted Caldwell, Pari's father

The best relationships are usually easy. Everything about them is simple. It's like slipping your hand into a glove. It's like a freight train going full steam ahead. A relationship should consist of chemistry, laughter, lots in common, and loads of great times.

If you're experiencing tears, arguments, and misunderstandings, your hurt feelings should signal there's something wrong. If it's too much work, the relationship won't work. Even if you try to force it, it still won't work. It's better to end things quickly and stop wasting your time.

"*I never hated a man enough to give him back his diamonds.*"

—Zsa Zsa Gabor, actress

If a man gives you presents and you end up going your separate ways, don't give them back! It would be bad manners and you wouldn't want to be rude, would you?

Gifts should have no strings attached. Legally they belong to you, and chances are, if you spent much time with him, you probably deserved every bling and bauble, Escada, and Chanel.

On the other hand if you are talking about an engagement ring, there are some protocols:

- **If the split was your idea,** you should return the ring.

- **If he broke the engagement,** the ring is yours.

- **In the case of a family heirloom,** the ring should be returned to the original owner's family.

If you're one of those who lost the guy but got the ring, think about recycling. Next time you're at a function for remarkably exciting singles, look at the stunning new clasps on Buffy's, Muffy's, and Cindy's pearls. They've discovered a trendy way to use their engagement rings. You can too.

Don't Break Out The Champagne Before It's Time

The next time you and your sweetheart are drinking a toast, remember not to get ahead of yourselves. Never let yourself think about marriage until you've been dating at least nine months. You both need that amount of time to make a proper decision.

It's unrealistic to expect a man who has been a bachelor for any length of time (particularly a man who has already failed at marriage) to make a decision quickly. Give him a year.

Have you ever poured a glass of champagne too quickly, only to have it bubble over? Or have you experienced a cork exploding right off the bottle before you finished opening it? Think of your relationship as being under that much pressure. You'll have more control if you take your time.

During your courtship when you share a glass of champagne with your lover, don't have too much. What you might say could spill over and ruin more than your blouse. Cheers!

Always Leave a Connection

—Put Livermore, Pari's husband

When a relationship finally comes to an end, it seems a shame to cut the cords completely. I'm not suggesting you string him along or drag out the relationship once it's finished. When it's over it's over. But skip the dramatic exits. He's learned so much about you and you've learned so much about him, why let the time you invested in one another go to waste? If possible turn him into a friend.

> *Why let the time you invested in one another go to waste?*

When you end your relationship, don't throw a fit or make hurtful remarks. Be gracious and thank him for the fun you've had together. If you are appreciative it will be easier to remain friends.

You never know what could happen in the future. He could always rope you back in or he might just introduce you to the love of your life.

My friend Tom dated Bobbie, a flight attendant, for several months. When it was time for their breakup, she was especially gracious. When Gerry, one of Tom's clients, came into town, Tom introduced him to Bobbie. They were married the following year.

go:

How to
Close
The Deal

Getting to the "M" Word

There are wonderful women walking around who've never worn a wedding ring because they couldn't close a deal. Many of them dated a man for two, three, or even five years. The honey was usually out of the moon by the time they grew fed up enough to ask, "When are we getting married?"

Usually a man won't decide to marry until he's nudged into it. Some women think, "I don't want to push. I want him to be sure." About 65 percent of all the married men I know needed a push to be sure.

The phrase "Ultimatums don't work with me" can intimidate any woman. It means: "It's been the wrong girl or the wrong time."

If every woman waited until the man thought it was the right time to propose, the birthrate would decline sharply. Most men don't propose unless there's a change in the relationship or they receive an ultimatum. I know many women who've gotten what they wanted. Here's how they did it (read on for details):

- Became indispensable

- Made major life changes

- Used "The Velvet Hammer."

Become
Indispensable

I once met a stranger on an airplane. We talked about the man I was dating who happened to be dragging his feet about getting married. As strangers sometimes do he decided to give me a little advice. "Women aren't too smart," he said. "If I were a woman, I could get any man to marry me!" He proceeded to explain. "A giving woman can make herself indispensable," he promised. "She should think of little things she can do to make a man happy and then do them."

Accentuate the skills you have so you may show them off to your greatest advantage. Try to figure out how you can best impact your man's life. If he and his neighbor want to have a dinner party for some of their friends, and you're great in the kitchen, cook for them. If he loves to play tennis and you can play, lob some balls at him. If you pass his dry cleaners on the way to your office, pick up his dry cleaning. While you're at it any kindness you can show him, any compliment you can give him, do it.

Make him wonder what he would ever be able to do without you. But don't mention the word marriage! "When you think it's time for him to propose, try withdrawing," the stranger said. "If you've made yourself truly indispensable, he won't be able to let you go."

I never got a chance to thank my seating companion for his words of wisdom, which I have since passed along to many women who became brides.

Use The
Velvet
Hammer

If you're over 30, one year is the perfect amount of time for both of you to decide about your future. By then if he has not proposed, you need to tell him how you feel. Be sweet and understanding, straightforward and honest. Don't cry, rant, and rave, or be otherwise unpleasant. If he's going to marry you, he'll want to know you can talk over decisions calmly. Tell him gently you want to marry him and let him know how much you love him.

Explain that it's time for him to propose and give him less than a month. Tell him gently that you cannot continue the relationship unless the two of you decide to get married. When having this discussion try to emulate the most elegant and gracious woman you have ever known, but be strong. The velvet is in your approach; the hammer is in your resolve.

All this may surprise him. If you've been smart you may never have spoken about marriage. He may be in shock, but he'll welcome the time you've given him to decide. While he's deciding, try not to mention marriage—and make it the best month he's ever had.

Getting married may be frightening to him. He will do everything he can to bribe you, persuade you, or bully you into giving an extension. Don't fall for this. The hammer part is as important as the velvet part. Thank him for your wonderful time together and walk away quietly and confidently.

If the deadline passes but you continue to date him without becoming engaged, he'll probably never marry you. He'll certainly never believe you mean what you say. If you continue to see him, his regard for you will be lessened because he'll think you're just another woman who succumbed to his charms. If you use The Velvet Hammer and it doesn't work, your relationship will never be the same. It should end.

The Velvet Hammer is a win-win. If he decides to marry you, the "Wedding March" will be in your future. If he decides not to marry you, you'll have saved yourself a lot of time.

Many men will not be able to make a decision within the allotted time. The loneliness of living without you may take time to sink in. After a few days, weeks, or months, men often realize what they've lost and finally propose. Hopefully you will not have met someone else by then. I have observed many women who used ultimatums successfully. I saw what worked and what didn't. Eventually I coined The Velvet Hammer.

Often when I meet someone new, she will take me aside and whisper, "My sister just got married and she used The Velvet Hammer." This technique has become so identified with me, when I meet someone they will say, "I'm glad to meet you. Tell me about this hammer thing."

Before my associate became engaged, she explained to her mother in Russia that she intended to give the American man I introduced her to an ultimatum. I laughed when I heard that her mother had phoned and inquired whether her daughter had used The Velvet Hammer.

And that came all the way from Khabarovsk in the Russian Far East. I have taught many women to use it successfully. I know it works.

There'll Be Some Changes Made

If you're too shy to hit a man with The Velvet Hammer, you might want to try something else first. Many men won't get married unless there are big changes in your relationship—such as those caused by the following events:

• Moving, or completing college or military service

• Getting a new job so you have much less time for each other

• Having demanding family emergencies such as illness or death

• Loss of interest on your part.

If a man doesn't come after you when any of these changes occur, it's usually not a good sign. However some men may be quite dense and think these changes are only temporary. They won't respond quickly enough. For those, there's always The Velvet Hammer!

"If you meet a woman you like and she's in between men, grab her—with the good ones you've only got about fifteen minutes."

—Edward Addison Dent, business leader and friend of Pari

If a guy tells you you're not the one, don't pout. Hit the pavement running. Scores of exciting men are eager to meet you. Even if your heart is broken, try to connect with a new man. It may happen more quickly than you think.

Take Bobbie, an attractive pharmacist with a dynamite smile, who fell for Lou, an oral surgeon from Buffalo. After two years of dating,

Bobbie teased Lou by humming the old cowboy tune: "On top of Old Smoky, all covered with snow, I lost my true lover by courting too slow."

Lou didn't take the hint, and Bobbie finally gave him an ultimatum.

Afterward he disappeared for several months. And then one rainy spring evening Lou showed up at Bobbie's door with a 3-karat diamond engagement ring in a velvet box. She was kind but said she couldn't talk. Her new boyfriend, Adam, was sitting on the couch eating a bowl of popcorn. Lou didn't quite understand it was too late and he tried to push his way into the apartment. But Adam very protectively closed the door.

Bobbie claimed the incident pushed Adam into action, and five months later they married. When Lou heard about the wedding, he sent a gift, a well-framed print of the Great Smoky Mountains.

Although it's been a decade, Lou remains unmarried and his friends claim he refers to Bobbie as "the only girl I ever loved." Every Christmas he receives a photo of Bobbie and Adam with their two sons and a cocker spaniel named Sam.

Photographers